Chickens on the Farm

by Mari C. Schuh

Consulting Editor: Gail Saunders-Smith, Ph.D.

Consultant: Cary J. Trexler, Ph.D., Assistant Professor
Department of Agricultural Education and Studies
Iowa State University

Pebble Books

an imprint of Capstone Press
Mankato, Minnesota

MS CS MT TL ER CS ET EG

Pebble Books are published by Capstone Press
151 Good Counsel Drive, P.O. Box 669, Mankato, Minnesota 56002
http://www.capstone-press.com

1 2 3 4 5 6 07 06 05 04 03 02

Library of Congress Cataloging-in-Publication Data
Schuh, Mari C., 1975–
    Chickens on the farm / by Mari C. Schuh.
    p. cm.—(On the farm)
    Includes bibliographical references (p. 23) and index.
    ISBN 0-7368-0991-0
    1. Chickens—Juvenile literature. [1. Chickens.] I. Title. II. Series.
SF487.5 .S43 2002
636.5—dc21
                                              00-012707

Summary: Simple text and photographs present chickens and how they are raised.

Note to Parents and Teachers

The series On the Farm supports national science standards related to life science. This book describes and illustrates chickens on the farm. The photographs support early readers in understanding the text. The repetition of words and phrases helps early readers learn new words. This book also introduces early readers to subject-specific vocabulary words, which are defined in the Words to Know section. Early readers may need assistance to read some words and to use the Table of Contents, Words to Know, Read More, Internet Sites, and Index/Word List sections of the book.

10.95

Table of Contents

tail

comb

beak

wattle

feathers

wing

legs

Chickens are small
farm animals.

6

Most chickens live indoors on large farms.

8

Some chickens live
in coops on small farms.

Some farmers raise chickens for their meat.

Some farmers raise chickens for their eggs.

Farmers feed chickens grain and water.

Chickens peck
at their food.

Female chickens
are called hens.
Hens cluck.

Male chickens
are called roosters.
Roosters crow.

Words to Know

cluck—a sound that hens make; female chickens sometimes cluck to call their young.

coop—a small building that houses chickens

crow—a loud, crying noise; roosters often crow in the morning.

egg—an oval or round object that has a shell; young animals develop inside the shell; machines and people collect eggs from female chickens.

grain—the seed of a cereal plant; farmers feed chickens grain such as corn; farmers also feed chickens soybeans, vitamins, and minerals.

meat—the flesh of an animal that can be eaten

peck—to strike or to pick at something

raise—to care for animals as they grow and become older

Read More

Bell, Rachael. *Chickens.* Farm Animals. Chicago: Heinemann Library, 2000.

Miller, Sara Swan. *Chickens.* A True Book. New York: Children's Press, 2000.

Saunders-Smith, Gail. *Chickens.* Animals: Life Cycles. Mankato, Minn.: Pebble Books, 1997.

Internet Sites

Chickens Printout
http://www.enchantedlearning.com/subjects/birds/printouts/Chickenprintout.shtml

Kids Farm
http://www.kidsfarm.com

Top Livestock
http://www.usda.gov/nass/nasskids/games/topstck/Tpstock.htm

Index/Word List

animals, 5
cluck, 19
coops, 9
crow, 21
eggs, 13
farm, 5, 7, 9
farmers, 11,
  13, 15
feed, 15

female, 19
food, 17
grain, 15
hens, 19
indoors, 7
large, 7
live, 7, 9
male, 21
meat, 11

most, 7
peck, 17
raise, 11, 13
roosters, 21
small, 5, 9
some, 9,
  11, 13
water, 15

Word Count: 59
Early-Intervention Level: 8

Credits

Heather Kindseth, cover designer; Heidi Meyer, production designer;
  Kimberly Danger, photo researcher

David F. Clobes, Stock Photography, 14
Martin Rogers/Pictor, cover
PhotoDisc, Inc., 1, 20
Photo Network, 12
Photri-Microstock, 4, 16
Pictor, 18
Visuals Unlimited/Inga Spence, 6, 10; Warren Stone, 8